If you can truthfully answer 'yes' to all these questions, the next thing is to borrow a book from your library describing fully the needs of the pet you would like to keep. Study it carefully to make quite sure you know all about it, then wait a week or so to see whether you still feel it is the right one. If you are quite sure, go ahead.

Note for parents: *Never give a pet as a present unless you have considered it well in advance. You must be certain that the animal will be both happy and well looked after.*

George Cansdale

Acknowledgments

The photographs on pages 5, 10, 13, 17, 19, 27, 29 (bottom), 37, 41, 43, 45, 49 and 51 are reproduced by permission of Cyrus Andrews of the Tourist Photo Agency; the cover and photographs on pages 12, 16, 23, 25, 33, 35, 39 and 47 are by Tim Clark; the photograph on page 21 is by Eric Hosking O BE, Hon F R P S, F I I P; photographs on pages 9 and 15 are by John Moyes, pages 29 (top) and 31 by Laurence E. Perkins, editor of Aquarist and Pond-keeper, *and page 7 by Popperfoto.*

The publishers also wish to thank the People's Dispensary for Sick Animals for their advice, and the many Leicestershire people who were kind enough to allow their pets to be photographed.

Pets

by GEORGE CANSDALE BA, BSc, FLS

Ladybird Books Ltd   Loughborough   1977

Donkeys

Donkeys are clever and patient – and they are certainly not stupid. Their first homeland, long before they became working animals, was in the stony deserts of north-east Africa, where they had not only to be sure-footed but also able to live on poor food, with little to drink at some seasons.

Abraham and the other early Israelites used donkeys to carry their baggage long before they had camels or horses. The women also rode on donkeys with the men walking alongside.

In Britain not many donkeys work for a living, except perhaps to give rides at the seaside, but in countries around the Mediterranean they sometimes pull little two-wheeled carts, or carry such huge bundles of branches or hay that they are almost hidden.

A donkey makes a good and faithful pet that will give you many hours of pleasure riding it, but only if you have a small field or paddock, with a little shed where it can shelter in very cold weather. Most of the time it can stay outside, because it grows a thick winter coat, and it will find much of its food in the paddock and on the hedges. Even so, it must have some hay and oats (which are quite expensive) as well as water and attention all the year round. It enjoys a good brushing and sometimes its hoofs must be trimmed.

Ponies

There are several different kinds of pony, such as Exmoor, New Forest and Welsh. Best known of all is the tiny Shetland pony which first came from the islands far to the north of Scotland. All horses and ponies are measured in *hands* of 4 inches (10 cm) so that a pony of 10 hands, for example, is 40 inches or just over 1 metre, measured at the shoulder.

Even the smallest pony costs much more to keep than a donkey because it must have better food. Like a donkey, too, it must have a paddock for grazing and exercise, as well as a little stable and lots of attention. So most of us cannot have one of our own, especially if we live in towns. Fortunately there are many riding schools, where people are taught to ride properly, and Pony Clubs, where you meet other riders and learn all about looking after ponies.

All members of the horse family, which include donkeys and ponies, have horny hoofs which are wonderful for running on and grow all the time. If a pony has too soft a paddock its hoofs will not be worn down enough and the farrier or vet will have to come and trim them back to the right size and shape. If you ride a lot on hard paths and roads, however, the hoofs wear down very quickly, which is why specially made iron shoes must be fixed to them and changed fairly often.

Donkeys, ponies and horses must have head collars to control them. Saddles and harness are required if you ride, and these need quite a lot of care.

Alsatians

If you spoke of an Alsatian almost anywhere outside Britain few people would know you were talking about a popular dog, because mostly it is known by its proper name of German Shepherd dog. Like so many pet breeds it began as a working dog, helping shepherds in the hills of Germany and eastern France to look after their sheep. Many are still used in this way.

Although the Alsatian may look more like a wolf than most of our other breeds, in fact all dogs came from wild wolves long, long ago, when they were the very first animals to become friendly with humans.

Today we know the Alsatian for several jobs that it does wonderfully well. It is a splendid assistant to the police, and makes a fine Guide Dog for the Blind. It is often the winner in Obedience Tests at Dog Shows: long, patient training is needed for all of these and the Alsatian has just the right nature for it. Perhaps the most amazing test of all is when an owner's handkerchief or glove is mixed up with others, and the Alsatian picks it out at once. We could not detect any difference but the Alsatian has a very accurate nose; it can remember the exact smell it is looking for and pick it out. A dog's ears, too, are more sensitive than ours so that it can recognise its master's car long before anybody has heard a noise.

Don't forget that all dog owners must have an annual licence to keep a dog. The cost is only 37½p a year at present, but this may be increased shortly.

9

Labrador Retrievers

Labradors are famous for their obedience, and they are one of the best breeds for training as Guide Dogs for the Blind. Not all kinds learn as well as they do, of course, but every dog should be taught to obey. This is not because we can then enter our pet for the Obedience Class at a Dog Show, or because they will be nicer around the house. It is because an obedient dog is *safe*, both for itself and for people. A dog that does not answer commands, and runs into the road, can easily be killed or cause a bad accident.

So whatever kind of dog we have, we should give it some simple training or perhaps take it to the classes that are held in many towns. First of all, teach it to walk at heel instead of dragging you along; then to sit

when told, especially on the edge of a busy road before crossing. Some owners think their dogs are so well behaved that they can go on roads without a lead, but it is far better to keep the lead on until you come to a park or open space. Obedience is just as important in the country, as well, where a dog must learn to come immediately it is called.

Of course, Guide Dogs are something very special. Only a few dogs are good enough to do this wonderful job, becoming new eyes to a blind man and leading him safely to and from his home. Since owner and dog must learn to work in partnership, they spend a month together at the Guide-dog Training School, when the blind person also learns to look after his dog.

Poodles

Although these dogs used to be called French poodles, some people believe they first came from Germany. Now you can see them everywhere, in many colours, but mostly black, grey, white or brown.

At first poodles were big dogs used for hunting; this is the size we call standard today. With their thick curly coats they could run through bushes without being hurt, while their dense fur kept them warm when they went into water to fetch ducks that had been shot.

For modern houses and flats the smaller sizes are more convenient – the miniature and the toy. (A toy poodle is one which is under eleven inches – 28 cm – high at the shoulder, and a miniature is under fifteen inches – 38 cm.) Many people say that poodles are the cleverest of all breeds; they can learn many tricks, which they seem to find great fun.

If you let a poodle's wool grow, it nearly reaches the ground, so if you have a poodle somebody will have to spend quite a lot of time grooming it, or will have to pay to have it clipped. The poodle in the picture on the left has been prepared for a

show with what is called the lion clip. Most pet poodles have a simple cut called the lamb trim, and this can be done at home. Poodles do not shed hair, and are thus less trouble in the house.

Poodles have to have more time spent on them than many breeds, but every dog needs regular attention to coat and feet, as well as food and exercise every day of the year, including holidays!

Boxers

The Boxer is a German-bred dog; it has no connection with the British Bulldog although it looks quite similar. Boxers usually have their tails *docked* (cut quite short), but efforts are being made to stop tail-docking in Britain.

The Boxer is one of the most powerful dogs kept as pets, with a thick muscular neck. To control it you will need a strong 'choke chain' which can be bought at any Pet Store. This is much more effective than a collar because the harder the dog pulls, the more the chain tightens. The dog very soon learns not to pull.

It is specially necessary to teach these big dogs proper road drill. Whenever possible use a zebra crossing and wait for a moment while the dog sits, even if it would be safe to cross at once. A dog should never be out on its own, but if ever this does happen by accident a dog properly trained in kerb drill may use the crossing and be safe.

Many dogs live in flats without gardens so they have to take most of their exercise on pavements. This is where another bit of obedience training is needed. Don't allow your dog to soil the pavement; teach him to use the gutter.

If you choose a dog like a Boxer, remember that a big dog creates quite a lot of work, since it needs a great deal of exercise. It also eats more food than a smaller animal, making it more expensive to keep.

Terriers

Many years ago the fox terrier was a hard-working little dog that lived up to its name. It was expert at catching rats and rabbits, and went into the earths to drive out foxes. It gradually became more and more popular until at last it was only a pet; for several years it was top dog among all the many different breeds and it was no longer much used to help farmers and game-keepers.

Fox terriers were only one of many kinds of terriers, from the biggest of all, the black-and-tan Airedale, to tiny dogs like the Yorkshire terrier, below, that fits easily into a shopping basket. Although even today many terriers are excellent at catching rats, mice and rabbits, most now live in towns and are simply pets.

Another terrier has now become well known as a working dog. This dog is shorter than the true fox terrier and just the right shape for running under bushes and going down holes. It is called the Jack Russell terrier, or sometimes the Parson Jack Russell, because it was first bred by a country clergyman.

If you have a terrier – in fact, any kind of dog,

big or small – be especially careful when you go for a picnic or a walk in the country. After a car journey your dog will want a run, but never let it out of your sight. Unless you are in a park or common where dogs are allowed to run free it is best to keep it on a lead. A dog can easily get lost, particularly on ground it does not know. It can also get excited and start chasing sheep, and get into serious trouble with a farmer.

Pigeons

Tame pigeons are in many colours, but most are the same shape as their wild cousins, the rock doves. They are powerful fliers; sometimes they make their nests in rocky hills in deserts or on tall sea cliffs and then fly long distances each day to find food and water for their chicks.

The Romans were the first people to send messages by pigeon post, and pigeons are still sometimes used in this way. The message is written on a tiny piece of paper and fixed under the wing or on a leg. Many pigeons also have one or more rings on their legs so that they can be identified. Of course we cannot tell pigeons to take a message just anywhere but they have a strong homing instinct and will fly straight back to their own homes, or lofts as they are usually called. They are put in special baskets and taken some distance from home, then released.

Gradually the distance is increased on each training flight, and when they are fully trained, pigeons can return safely even from 500 miles (800 kilometres) away.

Instead of carrying messages pigeons now fly in races, and special clocks are used to show the exact time that the birds get back home.

When racing, a special removable ring is attached to the pigeon's leg. When the pigeon returns to its own loft, the ring is taken off and put in a 'thimble' – a small tube about an inch (2.5 cm) long which comes apart. The 'thimble' is inserted in a hole in the clock case, a lever is turned and the time is registered on a paper dial. The

pigeon's speed can then be worked out. A pigeon is not considered to be 'home' until it has gone through the trap of its loft.

Many pigeons get lost and join the flocks living in cities. They seem to think that the tall buildings are cliffs and the window ledges made for nesting on. Pigeons usually lay only two eggs.

Fantail Pigeons

The common pigeons are the working birds, stream-lined and fast-flying. There are also many other varieties of tame pigeon; most of these are not at all like the wild rock dove of our sea cliffs from which they have all come. Some are very strange, like the tumbler pigeon that falls over and over in the air, and the pouter pigeon, which blows up its crop until the pigeon's head is almost buried in it. The fantails are very elegant, and these are probably the best variety to keep if you have room for them.

They live happily in a dovecot made from an old barrel or box which should be put on a pole where they will be safe from cats. They can be shut up at night and allowed to fly by day. All tame pigeons eat some green stuff but seeds like maize, wheat and field peas form their main food. These seeds are hard so the pigeons also swallow pieces of sharp grit to help grind them in their strong stomachs, called gizzards.

Before you decide to keep pigeons, work out how much the food will cost, at about two ounces (57 g) a day for each bird. They are also going to do some damage to your garden and, even worse, to your neighbours' gardens. Although they lay only two eggs and feed their babies in the nest for a month, they can have several families in the year and a pair of fantails can soon become about ten!

Barbary Doves

This pretty little dove is usually called the Barbary dove because it comes from North Africa. It is a smaller cousin of the beautiful turtle dove that is the latest of all our summer bird visitors to arrive.

Another close relation is the collared dove that is now so common in towns and villages and wakes us up with a call that sometimes sounds like a cuckoo.

The Barbary dove was first tamed a very long time ago: it could easily be the same turtle dove that is often mentioned in the Bible. Like all doves and pigeons it feeds its young on food prepared in its own crop (sometimes called 'pigeon's milk').

The parents take turns sitting on the eggs, which hatch in about seventeen days. The nestlings grow quickly. In two weeks they start to get proper feathers; after another fortnight they are as big as their parents and ready to fly.

These doves are usually kept in an aviary, since they may get killed if they are allowed to fly around freely. The aviary should be not less than about 2 metres (2 yards) in each direction. (Obviously, the bigger it is, the

better.) It should have several wood perches and a little bit of branchy tree where the doves can build their nest of twigs.

Like the bigger fantails and racing pigeons, these doves learn to come to the hand for food but very few birds really enjoy being actually held, and you should avoid doing so, if possible.

Tabby Cats

Cats are often said to belong to the house while dogs attach themselves to the people living there. Sometimes a cat that has been taken with a family moving house may decide to walk back to its old home, a journey that may take days or even weeks.

Cats started living with people very long ago: it all began in Ancient Egypt, perhaps around the time when the Pyramids were being built. In those days Egypt was famous for its corn, which farmers stored in special buildings called granaries. Rats and mice came to steal the corn from these big stores; the wild cats moved in to catch them, so the farmers encouraged the cats and they gradually became tame.

Some of these wild cats still live in countries around Egypt and they look rather like our tabby cat. Now there are many other varieties and if you go to a Cat Show you will be surprised to see how many different colours and shapes there are. There is even one with a curly coat, called a *Rex* cat.

Most of our pets are short-haired, like this tabby, and this is really the best type for the ordinary home, since a short coat is easy to keep in good condition. Persian cats, with their long, thick fur, need daily grooming, although all cats must be brushed often, since dirty coats encourage fleas and lice. The cat's bedding must also be kept clean. Whatever cat we choose, we must give it proper food and water regularly. Its ears must be inspected from time to time to keep them clean, and its claws must not be allowed to grow too long.

Siamese Cats

Siamese are town cats and it is hard to think of them going out into the fields to hunt for mice. Nobody is quite sure where their first home was, but it does seem that they have come to us from Siam, where they were regarded as royal animals. With short smooth hair, pale body and dark feet, face, ears and tail the Siamese is a very good looking cat, with beautiful blue eyes.

In some ways Siamese seem rather more like dogs though, of course, they are true cats in every way. For instance, they attach themselves to people rather than to the home, and they enjoy going for walks or in the car. They have quite a different voice from other cats, not a miaow, and they are very talkative. Some Siamese cats also like watching television, especially animal programmes, and others, surprisingly, like to go for a swim.

The Seal point Siamese shown on the right is the kind most people know. ('Points' are darker ears, paws, tail and face mask.) There are however Chocolate, Lilac, Blue, Red and even Tabby point Siamese, like the one on the left.

26

Their short coats need little attention for they can never get into a tangle, but Siamese cats must be looked after properly, just like any other kind. Sometimes they may enjoy a few table scraps but it is much better to give regular food, either tinned or cooked. Twice a day, at about the same times, give just as much as they can finish up. Siamese hardly ever drink milk; they must always have a bowl of clean water.

Goldfish

The Chinese began keeping goldfish many hundreds of years ago. The wild goldfish was a member of the carp family (something like those that live in our ponds and lakes, which can grow to over 40 lb (18 kg). The Chinese are expert fish keepers and they have bred many different varieties, some with strange names like comet-tail and veil-tail, with long waving fins and tails. These are sometimes rather difficult to look after, and it is best to start with just ordinary goldfish, like the one opposite.

Keeping goldfish in glass bowls is not a very good idea because only one small fish can live in a bowl, and it is not easy to keep the water clean and fresh. Goldfish can live in garden ponds but if you want one indoors it is better to get a small tank, which must have plants in it to help to keep the tank clean and fresh. It does not need any heating. The window is a good place for the tank, but it should not be in strong sunlight. A small electric bulb over the tank is good for the plants and shows up the fish better, but it is not essential.

Goldfish are fed mainly on a dry food that is bought in packets, but fish need little food and it is easy to give too much. A good rule is to feed once a day, with only as much as they eat while you watch. Anything that is left over goes bad and spoils the water. You can sometimes vary their diet with insects and worms, for they enjoy these.

A well-planned tropical fish tank
with plenty of plants

Tropical Fish

There are many kinds of tropical fish and if you go to a Tropical Aquarium shop you will probably see at least fifty different sorts. Barbs, swordtails, guppies and catfish (that keep the bottom of the tank clean) are amongst the most common.

Keeping tropical fish is a splendid hobby. They are bright and attractive, and several different kinds can live happily together. A tank does not take up much room and it looks interesting and attractive in the living room. Once a tank is properly established, it is simple to run and only needs to have rubbish cleaned from the bottom about once a week. No matter what sort of fish you keep, however, you must have a tank with fittings and plants, and together these cost quite a lot. Then there is electricity for lighting and keeping it warm, and the problem of holidays, so it really is something to talk over carefully before starting.

If you decide to go in for tropical fish the best thing is to ask an expert about it first of all. You can watch all the different things he has to do and learn something of the problems as well as the fun.

Guppies, mollies and swordtails are good kinds to start with, for they are both cheap and easy to look after, as well as being brightly-coloured.

Top   *Harlequin fish*
Centre *Zebra fish*
Bottom *Golden Barbs*

Dutch Rabbits

Although there are now so many different kinds of tame rabbit, they have all come from the wild rabbit that we see in the fields and woods. You can choose from many colours and patterns, long, short or curly coats, short ears or long ears. The tiniest weighs only 3 lbs (1.3 kg) and the biggest about 20 lbs (9 kg), which is much too big for a pet.

The Dutch rabbit is a favourite. Perhaps it first came from Holland but its name now refers to the regular pattern of black or brown on the head and body that makes it look so neat.

Rabbits enjoy being in a run in the garden in good weather, but for most of the time a hutch is better because they are safer there and easier to keep clean, especially if you put several thicknesses of newspaper on the floor and then cover with sawdust. The hutch must be cleaned out regularly, and the rabbit's droppings, along with the sawdust and newspapers, can go on the compost heap or be buried in the garden as manure.

If you do let your rabbit have a run on the lawn, make sure it is never left loose in the garden, for it can easily be lost and then killed. It can also do a lot of damage to the plants. Rabbits do not always get on well together and it is better to keep just one as a pet.

Netherlands Dwarf Rabbits

The two smallest kinds of rabbits also have foreign names. The Polish rabbit is not very common and is sometimes rather bad-tempered. The Netherlands Dwarf (which weighs about 3 lbs – 1.3 kg) is the friendliest rabbit you can ever find. It comes in many colours, but mostly black and grey, and has short, neat ears. Being so small it needs a smaller hutch than most kinds. It eats less and so does not make so many droppings, and it is just about the best breed to keep as a pet.

There are two different ways of feeding rabbits. If you live in the country and are willing to work a bit harder, they will do well on raw food: many kinds of greenstuff (both weeds and vegetable trimmings), roots (like peelings from carrots and turnips), and odd crusts of bread. They need hay to chew all the time, and if you make a little rack on the side or back of the hutch it can be pulled out a mouthful at a time and not wasted.

Many people, especially those who keep lots of rabbits, use a pellet food which is a balanced diet. Since it is rather concentrated, they need hay with it, and plenty of water to drink, from a little bottle fastened upside-down on the cage front that they soon learn to use.

When picking up a rabbit, steady it with one hand low down on the ears, then take the weight with the other hand under the back legs.

A white Netherlands Dwarf rabbit

Guinea Pigs

How wrong can a name be? Guinea pigs do not come from Guinea, which is part of West Africa, and they are certainly not pigs. Their original home was in Peru and when the first Spanish sailors went there over four hundred years ago, they found the Incas keeping them as pets. Guinea pigs (or *cavies* as they are often called) belong to the big family of gnawing animals, with front teeth that never stop growing and have to be kept short by hard wear.

Guinea pigs live in the same sort of hutch as rabbits but since they are smaller, it need not be so tall. They eat the same kind of food as rabbits and are looked after in the same way. They come in many colours – sometimes all black, brown or white, or one or even two colours with white. They have three kinds of coat: short-haired, rough-haired, and long-haired. The short-haired kind is best as a pet.

The mother guinea pig has to wait for ten weeks before the babies are born; they are fully furred, with eyes open at once. They run around and start nibbling food very soon, and go on having milk from their mother for about three weeks. Father and mother can usually live together all the time, even when the babies are born.

If your hand is big enough, pick up your guinea pig by putting your right hand over the shoulders, with thumb and forefinger around the neck. This steadies it while your other hand under the back feet takes the weight.

Rough-haired Guinea Pig

Short-haired Guinea Pigs

Canaries

The canary is still the best singer among all the birds we keep as pets. Many wild canaries are found in Africa but our tame birds all come from a greenish-yellow kind that lives in the Canary Islands, off the north-west coast of Africa.

Experts now recognise many different types of tame canary: some are all bright yellow, others have darker markings or are greenish, and they vary in size and shape. Roller canaries are the best singers and they go on for minutes at a time. They make up some tunes of their own but usually they are taught by older birds.

Canaries belong to the finch family, with strong bills for cracking hard seeds to get out the kernels. You can buy just the right mixture to put in their food pots, and each day you should blow away the husks and fill up the pot again. They need clean water all the time and they also enjoy nibbling some greenstuff such as groundsel and seeding grasses, or a bit of apple.

The floor of the cage should be sprinkled with fine sand, but you can, if you wish, buy sanded paper from a pet shop which makes it easier to clean out the cage. From time to time take out the canary and give the cage a thorough wash, putting mild disinfectant in the water you use. Scrub the wooden perches well and when they get worn or rough renew them with a piece of dowelling (you can buy this from a do-it-yourself shop).

Canaries like to be in the living room but if the cage is in the window make sure it is not in strong sunlight or in a draught.

n from
ies are
arker
ocks
ing
ass
of

Budgerigars

The first budgies were brought to Brita[in] Australia over a hundred years ago. Wild bud[gies] mostly green, with yellow on the head and some markings on the back and wings. They live in big [flocks] which fly around looking for grain fields and see[ding] grasses, which is why they are sometimes called g[rass] parrakeets. As the beak shows clearly, it is a member [of] the parrot family, but one of the smallest.

The budgie now comes in so many colours that even an expert can hardly know them all, but they are usually blue, green or yellow.

Any colour will make a good pet and most will learn to talk if you go about it the right way. Start with a young bird six or seven weeks old and not very long away from the nest, so that it is glad to have companionship. When a budgie talks or whistles it is only imitating what it has heard, so be patient and say the same word or phrase clearly over and over again. Budgies can be handled more easily than canaries – in fact, they seem to like sitting on a finger or shoulder and flying round the room (but make sure they can't fly into or onto a fire).

They do well on a budgie seed mixture but it is good to try several kinds and see which is least wasted. A budgie eats about 3 oz (85 g) a week as well as some greenstuff. Also give it a little grit block to help keep the beak worn – even with this the beak may grow too long and need to be trimmed by an expert. A budgie's claws too may sometimes need trimming.

Goats

If you wanted to see real wild goats at home you would have to visit some small islands near Greece and then go right up into the hills. Goats are great climbers and even when they are only a few days old they can jump from rock to rock. Some goats even learn to climb trees to get tasty leaves and twigs.

Goats have been useful animals for a very long time. In the Bible, you will read that Abraham and his family had huge flocks which provided many useful things: meat and milk; hair for weaving into cloth; skins that were made into leather and used for bottles, sandals, belts and so on.

Unfortunately goats can do terrible damage when allowed to roam because they eat all the small trees and shrubs. So if you keep a goat as a pet it must always be controlled. The best thing is to fit a strong collar with a chain fixed to it. The other end of the chain is pegged down and the goat moved to a new place every day, such as on the roadside or a common, but it should always have water available.

Another way is to fix a long wire in a field or orchard, then a ring on the end of the chain runs along the wire. This gives the goat some freedom while still keeping it under control.

Of course goats can be kept only in the country, for it would be very unfair to keep one without plenty of space and a shed for shelter in winter. Goats are kept

for milking (goat's milk is pure-white in colour and is easier to digest than cow's milk) and there are nearly as many different breeds as in cattle. Hospitals sometimes need goat's milk to treat patients with certain rare diseases.

Golden Hamsters

Although the first hamsters kept as pets really had a golden coat, there are now so many colours that perhaps we should just call them hamsters. Golden hamsters came from Syria in 1930 so it is one of the latest wild animals to become a popular pet.

A hamster is best kept in the living room, and if it is looked after properly there is little smell. Be careful not to let it stay outside or in a very cold corner in winter because it will go into a deep sleep from which it may not wake up. Hamsters are near-sighted, so when you go to pick one up put your hand in slowly. It is best to keep just one, because even a true pair will always be fighting.

Dog biscuit meal makes a good diet and a hamster eats about a dessertspoonful every day. Do not be surprised if food all disappears at once; the hamster has put it in its cheek pouches and carried it home to store away. Check this store from time to time to see if you are giving too much.

If a hamster has some vegetable or greenstuff every day, such as lettuce, cabbage, carrot or apple core, it gets plenty of moisture, but it still needs a small container of water. A hamster's droppings are small and dry, and always put in one corner, which makes the cage easy to keep clean.

To pick up a hamster safely put your hand over its back, with finger and thumb around the neck, but be careful not to hold too tight, and take the weight on your other hand.

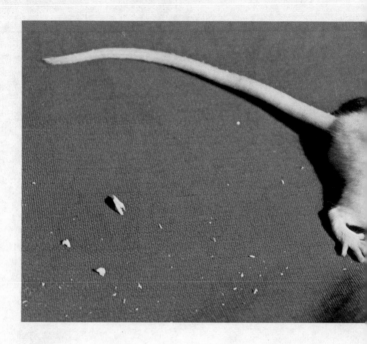

Mice

Though we often speak of keeping white mice it is really better to call them tame mice or fancy mice because we get them in black, white and browns, as well as mixtures of colours and in different patterns.

The wild mice from which all these tame mice have come had their home far away in Asia. Gradually they got carried around in goods and baggage until they reached Britain perhaps three hundred years ago.

Until hamsters came along these tame mice were very popular as pets but they have always had several disadvantages. They have a strong smell (the male is the

real trouble, so it is better to keep just females), and they are also expert at escaping.

Metal cages are better in some ways but are rather cold. If you use wood, paint the inside very thoroughly first and it will be easier to keep clean, especially if you use plenty of sawdust. Most mice are now fed on special pellets. You can also give the odd crust and table scrap, but don't over-feed. Mice need lots of water too.

To pick up a mouse, take the base of the tail firmly with finger and thumb, lift and put it down on the other hand, still steadying it gently by the tail.

Hedgehogs

A hedgehog makes a pet quite different from all the others in this book. It is better to look on it as a garden guest that lives around the place and sometimes takes food that we put out for it.

Hedgehogs belong to the same family as the active little shrews and the burrowing mole that can make such a mess of our lawns and gardens. They all feed on worms, slugs, insects and other 'creepy crawlies'. The hedgehog also catches and eats snakes, even the poisonous adder.

Usually a hedgehog becomes our guest rather by accident, when it moves into our garden and makes its home there. Or perhaps you may see one on the side of a busy road and feel it would be safer if you put it in your garden. You may hear or see them at night, but they hide away so well by day that they are usually impossible to find, even in a small garden.

If you know roughly where it lives, put down a saucer with a little brown bread and milk or a few meaty scraps. Give only a little, for hedgehogs will find most of their own food and help by keeping down garden pests. Don't try to handle it; just be glad that one lives in your garden and that you see it from time to time.

Hedgehogs sleep for part of the winter in a hole or deep down in a heap of leaves. It may be Christmas before they hibernate, and even when hibernating they may wake up for a few days if there is a warm spell.

Tortoises

The tortoises that we keep as pets have come from countries around the Mediterranean, so they are used to a different climate from ours. In their homeland they have a long hot summer when they are active and store away reserves of fat in their bodies to take them safely through their winter sleep, or hibernation.

Sometimes our summer is not really hot enough for them, so our tortoises come to the autumn with only just enough stores to get through to spring. Then perhaps the winter is not cold enough to make them sleep deeply, so they wake up for a bit and waste energy moving around.

So in the autumn we should pack the tortoise away carefully in a carton or box filled with straw and leaves and keep it in the coldest place that is protected from frost. Perhaps a garden shed or cellar (but not indoors) and you must make sure the box is rat-proof.

Let your tortoise have the run of the garden, but check that it cannot get under the fence or out of the garden gate and be lost or run over.

Tortoises have big appetites, but they can be fussy about food, some liking one sort of greenstuff or fruit and some another. In the garden they can mostly find what they need, but you may have to stop them from eating precious plants. In hot dry weather, give lettuce and cabbage leaves; make sure that the water bowl is full, and that they can get into shade.

Always turn over leaves and garden debris carefully before burning, in case of hibernating tortoises or hedgehogs

Never tie a string to a leg to stop your tortoise wandering; nor should you make a hole in its shell. A good plan is to paint its name on its shell – if you use luminous paint you will be able to spot your tortoise under bushes or in shadowy corners.

A tortoise that is looked after properly can live in your garden for twenty years or more.

INDEX